Top left: The sparkling waters of Agincourt Reef. *Top right:* Above the treetops on the Kuranda Skyrail.
Bottom left: Swaying palms at Palm Cove. *Bottom right:* The Marlin Marina and the Pier Marketplace.

THE MAGIC OF THE TROPICS

"The Tropics" conjures up images of sparkling clear waters, brilliantly coloured coral reefs and fish, and lush rainforest. In tropical north Queensland all these promises are kept. Today we are aware that, as well as providing adventure, the reefs and rainforests are among the most beautiful and fragile environments on earth. If the bounteous natural gifts of the region are treated with caution and respect, the visitor will be richly rewarded with unforgettable experiences of excitement and breathtaking beauty.

Above and opposite: Sunrise turns the tropical sea to liquid fire as people plunder its riches or simply enjoy its beauty.

CAIRNS

Cairns is the tourist capital of north Queensland. It is the jumping-off point for reef, rainforest, beaches, tableland and the outback. But it is much more than that—Cairns is the centre of diverse economic activity, including farming of sugar cane and tropical produce of all kinds. Tourism and industry mix harmoniously with the natural environment.

Cairns, like many other northern towns and cities, began as a port from which to ship timber, beef, gold and minerals from the inland. It lies in Trinity Bay, near the mouth of the Barron River. The population is a glorious mix of races and nationalities, from the original Djabuganydji people and the descendants of South Sea Islanders who were brought to work on the sugar fields, to post-war European immigrants.

Today, Cairns is an international gateway. It is an exciting city with world-class facilities, including a casino, restaurants, botanic gardens, shops, theatres and galleries to be enjoyed in tropical sunshine under clear blue skies.

Above: Trinity Bay offers a spectacular welcome to visitors flying into Cairns. *Left:* The Marlin Marina and the Pier Marketplace dominate this view of Cairns looking from Trinity Bay west to the Tableland.

Above: The Cairns Hilton, seen from above, with the casino directly behind.

Above: Trinity Wharf and the tourist ferry terminal, with the casino and Cairns city in the background.

LAZY DAYS

The Esplanade is central to the spirit of Cairns—it is a meeting place, but also a place where anyone can find solitude and relax in the sun. At low tide, birds hunt on the mudflats and dreamers on the shore watch them while joggers exercise, families stroll and holiday-makers catch their breath after a day on the reef. Just to the north lie sandy beaches fringed with palms, and everywhere the glistening peacock blues and greens of the sea cool the eye.

Top left: The cenotaph stands in memory of those from Cairns who went to war.
Top right: Despite the area's popularity, there is plenty of room to stretch out in the sun.
Bottom left: Dreaming on the Esplanade, looking south to the marina, casino and marketplace.
Bottom right: What more can life offer? *Opposite top:* Quiet, sandy beaches lie north of Cairns.
Opposite bottom: Looking north from Trinity Bay.

A THRIVING CITY

Cairns began as a sleepy port for shipping gold, tin and timber from the Atherton Tableland and the Hodgkinson River goldfield, and was even in danger of being overtaken by Smithfield, 12 kilometres to the north, or Port Douglas, yet further north. It has since grown to become a thriving modern city.

On Cairns's busy social calendar are, among other events, a two-day jazz festival in June, the Fun in the Sun festival in the second week of October, and a racing carnival in September. The Cairns Museum preserves local European and indigenous history, while the Freshwater Connection is a railway museum. The city also has a lively theatre and entertainment scene.

Cairns is a particularly wonderful place to shop — the Pier Marketplace, the City Place Mall, weekend markets, art galleries, bookshops, music shops, crafts, clothes and jewellery produced by local designers, Aboriginal art and artefacts ... there is so much to see and still more to buy.

Above: Cairns Convention Centre. *Left:* A view across Trinity Inlet to Cairns. *Inset, from left:* The Esplanade, City Place (interior and exterior), the Reef Hotel Casino.

WHEN THE SUN GOES DOWN

Soft, velvet tropical nights follow hot, sunny days. Gaming is popular at the casino, as well as spectacular live shows, restaurants and bars. In the city centre are nightclubs and live music venues. Restaurants of every type and cuisine are scattered throughout the city and suburbs, offering the opportunity to eat quickly before sampling the night-life, or dine leisurely while gazing at the water, the mountains or the lights.

Top: Cairns sparkles at night. Cape Grafton looms in the background across Trinity Inlet. *Opposite:* Along the Esplanade at night. *Right:* Architectural reminders of Cairns' early days add charm to the city.

FUN AFTER DARK

The restaurants of Cairns offer all styles of food—from modern Australian prepared by brilliant young chefs to classical Asian and European cuisines. Dining out in a city where so much heavenly food comes from the sea and where tropical fruits and vegetables thrive in the rich volcanic soil is bound to be a joy. The casino sparkles, inviting people to stop by, but it is just one of Cairns's night spots. Nightclubs and hotels welcome visitors for a meal, a drink, dancing or live music of most varieties. Cinemas and the Cairns Civic Theatre offer still more choices.

Opposite top: The Pier Marketplace lights up the evening. *Bottom left:* Dining alfresco on a balmy tropical night. *Bottom right:* Budget accommodation and dining are also in delightful settings. *Above:* The Reef Hotel Casino.

Top: A seaplane sits nudged into a berth in the marina next to the boats.   *Bottom:* The Pier Marketplace is an exciting place to shop at night.

Top and bottom: Splashes of colourful decorations, merchandise and people swirl inside the Pier Marketplace.

OUT TO THE CORAL SEA

Escaping to the reefs, islands and cays of the Coral Sea is a wonderful experience. Boats of all kinds are your passport to this magical World Heritage area. The beauty and diversity of the Great Barrier Reef has to be seen to be believed. A natural wonder of the world, the Reef is a complex structure made up of many reefs, and is home to about 1500 species of fish and about 400 types of coral.

Top: In the mornings the large cruise catamarans set off for day trips. *Bottom left:* A junk-rigged boat adds a touch of the exotic to the scene. *Bottom right:* History sits elegantly afloat—a square-rigger lies at its mooring. *Opposite:* Bare-boating or chartering allow exploration at your own pace, with the added fun of sailing.

A DAY ON GREEN ISLAND

Green Island is the closest island to Cairns. A classically teardrop-shaped coral cay, it lies north-east of Trinity Bay. Many day trips go to Green Island from Cairns, allowing visitors to view the reef from the underwater observatory, take trips in glass-bottom boats, and snorkel. It is an easy walk around the 12 hectare island to see the plant and bird life. Green Island also boasts a low-rise resort, and visits to Marineland Melanesia.

Left: Green Island's jetty stretches out to receive visitors.
Inset: Snorkelling in reef waters can open up a whole new world, such as seeing an anemonefish (centre) which lives unharmed in the stinging tentacles of a sea anemone.
Above: Bannerfish cruise close to the protecting reef—their home, shelter and source of food.

SAFARI TO MICHAELMAS CAY

North by north-east from Green Island is Michaelmas Cay and Michaelmas Reef, just over 50 kilometres from Cairns. Here the broad sweep of sea, sand and sky banish the cares of the workaday world.

Scuba diving and snorkelling on the reef are two of the main pastimes, but taking a reef walk at low tide is an absolute delight. Crabs, anemones and all manner of tiny sea creatures live dual lives—under water and above water. Tour guides advise on where to go, what to beware of and how to avoid damaging this fragile water garden. Michaelmas Cay is also an important breeding site for seabirds, such as Sooty Terns and Common Noddies.

Left: Surely nowhere on Earth has dancing water of such clarity as on the Reef. *Below:* Awed scuba divers drift near coral formations.

THE OUTER BARRIER REEF

Trips to the outer reef can last a day, or a week or more. The choice is yours, governed only by time and budget. This is serious diving territory—it really does not get any better. Hastings, Moore, Norman and Ribbon Reefs, the Cod Hole, Flinders Reef: the names have magic. Nonetheless, this whole area is very much more than a tourist playground. The Great Barrier Reef Marine Park is a large laboratory and research facility which aims to preserve and protect the reef and gain understanding of such creatures as the Crown of Thorns sea star which appear to be a threat.

Top left: Having some fun in the sun. *Top right:* Snorkelling is great, and you need little practice before you can really start exploring. *Bottom left:* The speedy tourist catamarans make nothing of distance. *Opposite:* Boats dot the reef surrounds while a large cruise boat is moored at the reef station.

BARRON GORGE

The Barron River tumbles down the Barron Gorge on its way from the Atherton Tableland to the coast. A trip on the Kuranda Scenic Railway, one of the greatest short railway journeys in the world, gives a spectacular view of the Falls and the Gorge. This is often the first glimpse of the northern rainforests that visitors get, and it gives an overview of the splendour of the forests and an idea of the massive geological time that went into creation of the landscape.

Left: The Kuranda railway station and its beautiful gardens are the perfect introduction to the Atherton Tableland.
Above: The magnificent Barron Falls at their awe-inspiring best.
Opposite: The Scenic Railway passes Stoney Creek Falls.

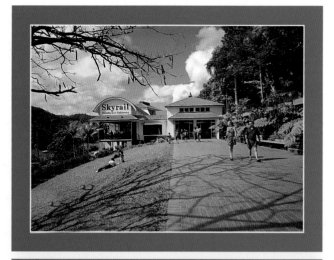

SKYRAIL THROUGH THE RAINFOREST

The Skyrail trip is the longest cable car journey in the world, swooping above the treetops for 7.5 kilometres between Smithfield and Kuranda. Many visitors to Kuranda travel one way by the railway and the other by the Skyrail. The cable car makes two stops on its way—once where travellers can walk to look out at the Barron Falls, and once at a rainforest interpretative centre. From the Skyrail, vistas of the coast and the tableland are spread out all round, as well as views of the forest canopy at close quarters.

Top: The Skyrail terminus at Kuranda. *Bottom:* Magnificent tree ferns nestle in the forest. *Left:* Soaring above the treetops.

KURANDA — VILLAGE IN THE RAINFOREST

Ever since the railway opened in 1891, sightseers have travelled from Cairns to Kuranda, a village steeped in history as well as being situated in an area of immense botanical and zoological significance. This peaceful, laid-back town begins to hum with activity on market days, and one can buy practically anything—from didgeridoos, bush saxophones, fine leatherwork and clothing to pottery, wooden toys, jewellery and basketware.

Above: Dense wet tropical rainforest surrounding Kuranda village. *Right:* The Kuranda markets where visitors can buy all manner of craft goods.

ABORIGINAL THEATRE

Smithfield is the home of the Tjapukai Dance Theatre, an internationally renowned local Aboriginal dance troupe. The performances explain a little of the indigenous culture as well as displaying the performers' dance skills. Close by Kuranda is Jilla Binna Crafts and Museum, where there is a further display of indigenous culture and some mementoes of the old Mona Mona mission.

Off the Kennedy Highway near Kuranda is the Rainforest Station, where visitors can take the Dreamtime Walk and see the Pamagirri Aboriginal Dancers perform. All of these artists are working to keep traditional tales alive, as well as creating contemporary dances to describe modern tribal life and experiences.

Above and left: Members of the Tjapukai Dance Theatre take delight in performing traditional and modern Aboriginal dances in full costume for visitors.

31

ENTER THE MAGIC RAINFOREST

Nothing can prepare the newcomer for the majesty of the wet tropics rainforests of north Queensland, and words simply cannot describe the awe visitors feel. Around the township of Kuranda are many walks through the forest and the residents have developed several parks and enclosed walks that help visitors view the less visible flora and fauna; for instance, the wildlife noctarium, where nocturnal animals such as gliders, larger possums, fruit bats and echidnas can be seen. The butterfly sanctuary is equally delightful. Sightseers can paddle canoes along the Barron River to experience the forest from the water.

Top: A male Dainty Green Tree Frog calls for a mate.
Bottom left: A male Australian King Parrot.
Bottom right: A Green Ringtail Possum. *Opposite:* The quiet beauty of the rainforest is an ideal antidote for the stress of the workaday world.

EXPLORING THE TABLELAND

The Atherton Tableland offers an equally beautiful but quieter life than the coastal region. Here are many farms, crater lakes such as Lakes Barrine and Eacham, Tinaroo Dam, national parks and wildlife reserves. To the west of the Tableland are historical mining towns like Herberton, the site of the original tin mines, and Chillagoe where copper, tin and silver-lead has been mined, and where gold and marble are still mined.

Top left: The lush pasture of the Tablelands. *Top right:* The Highlander Hotel, Mareeba, one of the old-style pubs that sprinkle the Tablelands. *Bottom left:* The Grand Hotel, Atherton, another historic hotel. *Bottom right:* Tourists inspect a Curtain Fig at Yungaburra. *Opposite:* Water cruises on Lake Barrine, a delightful way to see the spectacular vegetation and wildlife.

THE WORLD OF WATERFALLS

All of the rivers that rush from the Tableland to the narrow coastal plain freefall in places and tumble down boisterous rapids in other spots—the Tully, the Johnston, the Russell, the Mulgrave, the Barron, Mossman Gorge, the Daintree. The rainfall in the north is high, and even higher on the Tableland, much of which is some 900 metres above sea-level.

Left: The beautiful Nandroya Falls, Wooroonooran National Park. *Below:* Tchupala Falls, Wooroonooran National Park. *Opposite (clockwise from top left):* Elinjaa Falls, Atherton Tableland; Millstream Falls, Atherton Tableland; Josephine Falls, Wooroonooran National Park. *Following pages:* Millaa Millaa Falls, Atherton Tableland.

WILD WATER

Wherever the rivers of the north break into rapids free spirits can be found rafting the white water. For the ultimate experience of the thrill of pitting human skills, strength and endurance against the power of nature, there is little to match white water rafting, and the rivers of the wet tropics of north Queensland provide ideal conditions for this exciting sport.

Left and above: Whitewater rafting on the Tully River.

CANE FARMING

Sugarcane has been the faithful staple of the tropic north's economy. When the goldrushes of the late nineteenth and early twentieth centuries died away, most of the population grew to rely on the sugar industry for their livelihood. Towns were established to service canefarmers' needs, and people worked growing, cutting and milling cane, and then refining the sugar and making the many sugar byproducts.

Above: The canefields extend up into the hills behind the city of Cairns. *Top left:* Harvesting the cane. *Bottom left:* Seen from the air, the canefields form a magnificent countryside patchwork.

NORTH FROM CAIRNS

As travellers wend their way up the coast on the Cook Highway from Cairns, they will be treated to views of some of the most beautiful coastline in Australia. In many places it looks as if the mountains are tumbling into the clear water of the Coral Sea. Apart from Port Douglas, this is where the least heavily populated section of the Queensland coast begins.

Right: The Cook Highway snakes along the coastline south of Port Douglas. *Below:* The Bouncing Stones are an unusual geological formation along this stretch of coastline.
Following pages: Palm Cove, paradise on earth!

THE NORTHERN BEACHES

The beaches north of Cairns—Machans Beach, Holloways Beach, Yorkeys Knob, Trinity Beach, Clifton Beach, Palm Cove and Ellis Beach—are known as the Marlin Coast. They make pleasant stopping points on a leisurely trip to Port Douglas and points further north. Wide stretches of sand line much of the shore, and palms fringe these golden lips on the calm water. From Palm Cove it is only a few hundred metres to Double Island, a beautiful little island on which there is a luxury resort that can be reached by water taxi.

Opposite: Ellis Beach, where the mountains meet the sea. *Above:* Visitors relax under swaying palms on Clifton Beach.

PORT DOUGLAS

Port Douglas is the glamour capital of the north, now famous throughout the world as the place where even the US President can holiday safely and privately. Port Douglas was founded in 1877 as a port for the Hodgkinson River goldfield, and was named after John Douglas, a former premier of Queensland. It first hit the news in a big way with the building of the Sheraton Mirage, which was followed by the Radisson Royal Palms resort and a championship golf course which has hosted some memorable skins tournaments.

Despite all this, Port Douglas has kept its relaxed, low-key charm and there is still plenty of moderately priced accommodation for backpackers and families. It is an excellent stepping-off point for trips to the Low Isles, the Mossman Gorge, the Daintree, Cape Tribulation and the Reef, or Cape York and the Gulf.

Above: Luxury resorts are nestled into magnificent surrounds. *Left:* Yachts berthed at Marina Mirage. *Inset, from left:* Macrossan Street; Marina Mirage shopping centre; a walkway fringed by huge tree ferns.

Above: Four Mile Beach at Port Douglas has something for everyone—beach volleyball, spectacular scenery or just lazing in the sun.
Opposite: The sheltered waters off Four Mile Beach can tempt even the most inexperienced to try their hand at sailing.

A DAY AT LOW ISLE

A lighthouse dating from 1878 stands on this coral cay sitting within a surrounding lagoon where visitors have a chance to explore the magnificence of the Great Barrier Reef at close quarters. Sailboats, catamarans and large and small power boats all make their way to the Low Isles, where holiday-makers go snorkelling and diving, take trips in a glass-bottom boat, swim, or go for a guided walk with a marine biologist.

Top: Low tide gives visitors a chance to study the reef's many different forms of life. *Bottom:* An idyllic day on the beach. *Right:* The lighthouse rises from its surrounding vegetation. *Opposite:* The Quicksilver, with daytrippers aboard, edges toward anchorage.

MOSSMAN GORGE

Just 5 kilometres west of the town of Mossman, in the south of the World Heritage-listed Daintree National Park, lies the Mossman Gorge. It is impossible to look at the Gorge and not feel the awe that the first Europeans must have experienced when they stumbled on its primeval beauty. The water is always cool because it is shaded by the forest, and lichens, moss and ferns thrive on the rocks and in the crevices between them. Walking trails lead off from the carpark and, beyond the swimming holes, a suspension bridge carries walkers to a 2.5 kilometre circuit through the rainforest.

Fifty million years ago, almost all of Australia was covered in rainforest but, because of climate changes, nearly all of it had gone by the time the Aborigines arrived in Australia. Today, only about 20 000 square kilometres of rainforest is left, more than half in Queensland. The tropical rainforest has a special place in Australians' hearts, living as they do in a largely dry continent. Research continues so that we can enjoy and preserve the forests.

Above: The White-lipped Tree Frog may be spotted by vigilant hikers. *Right:* The wild Mossman River tumbles through the Gorge on its way to the sea.

DAINTREE RAINFOREST

Daintree, originally a logging town, lies east of the Daintree National Park, where some of the oldest forests in the world can be found. Bushwalking in the park is an unforgettable experience. The Daintree is one of the richest storehouses of plants and animals in the world, many species being found nowhere else, and scientists and nature lovers flock here to study and observe. The Daintree Rainforest Environmental Centre has been set up for visitors to learn more about the forest as they walk along self-guided boardwalks or watch films about the forest in the centre's theatre.

The Green Python (*top*) and the Herbert River Ringtail Possum (*bottom*) are some familiar inhabitants of the Daintree.
Left: The Daintree impresses visitors with its lush vegetation and its cathedral-like quietness.

DAINTREE RIVER

The Daintree is crocodile territory, and that means the dangerous saltwater crocodiles as well as the harmless freshwater species. These prehistoric saurians inhabit mangroves, coastal creeks and estuaries. Plenty of the saltwater breed can be seen in safety at the various crocodile farms and crocodile parks throughout the Top End, the Hartley Creek Crocodile Farm in the Daintree area being one of these.

Boat trips along the Daintree are an excellent way to see more of the forest and observe the local plant and wildlife. A boat trip is a blissfully relaxing alternative to walking the rainforest trails. The Alexandra Range Lookout offers panoramic views of the Daintree River's estuary and the national park.

Top: Dinner time for a Daintree salty. *Above left:* The 'Big Barramundi' tourist centre. *Left:* Exploring by boat. *Opposite (clockwise from top):* The estuary of the Daintree; Ulysses Butterfly; Cairns Birdwing Butterfly; Cooktown orchids, Queensland's floral symbol.

A VISIT TO CASSOWARY COUNTRY

In a forest of fan palms north of the Daintree River one of the two remaining cassowary colonies in Queensland can be found. (The other small colony is near Mission Beach, south of Cairns.) The cassowary is a large flightless bird, not as tall as the emu, but more heavily built. These birds are crucial in the forest because they are the only dispersal agents for some 70 plant species and the main dispersal agents for at least 30 more. This means that these seeds are spread by the cassowaries, which eat the fruit and then deposit the seeds in their droppings on the forest floor. A 1993 report from the CSIRO estimated that there were no more than 54 adult cassowaries left in this northernmost habitat. Although their numbers gradually reduced as their habitat shrank, feral animals such as pigs and wild dogs pose the greatest threat. These animals are very partial to cassowary egg for supper, and they will also kill young or ailing birds.

Above: A Southern Cassowary with chicks. Notice how the young's markings blend into the debris on the forest floor.
Right: A wide track in the palm forest.

A DAY AT CAPE TRIBULATION

Captain Cook named Cape Tribulation on one of his trips along Queensland's coast when he feared he may never get away from the reefs and back into deep water. The region's unique value and beauty was acknowledged when the Cape Tribulation National Park, spreading from the Daintree to the Bloomfield River, was declared in 1981.

Top left: A palm-fringed beach near the Cape. *Top right:* Cape Tribulation from afar. *Bottom left:* Glimpse of the sea between forest giants. *Bottom right:* Trunk of the Bumpy Satin Ash. *Opposite (clockwise from top left):* Part of the coastline seen from the road; a lone mangrove on the shore—most fish species rely on mangroves for their nurseries; an aerial shot of the Cape in all its splendour.

First published by Steve Parish Publishing Pty Ltd, 1997
PO Box 2160, Fortitude Valley BC, Queensland 4006, Australia

ISBN 1 875932 90 9

Photography: Steve Parish
  Photographic assistance: Phillip Hayson, SPP
  p. 31 © Tjapukai
  p. 59 Belinda Wright
  p. 60 Stan Breeden
Text: Wynne Webber
Editing: Carol Campbell, Bookmark Publishing
Design, art and film production: SPP
Printed in Australia